SPIDERS
Worldwide Webs

SPIDERS
Worldwide Webs

TAIT HOWARD

First Second
New York

:01
First Second

Copyright © 2021 by Tait Howard

Published by First Second
First Second is an imprint of Roaring Brook Press,
a division of Holtzbrinck Publishing Holdings Limited Partnership
120 Broadway, New York, NY 10271

Don't miss your next favorite book from First Second! For the latest updates
go to firstsecondnewsletter.com and sign up for our enewsletter.

Library of Congress Control Number: 2020910689

Paperback ISBN: 978-1-250-22283-1
Hardcover ISBN: 978-1-250-22284-8

Our books may be purchased in bulk for promotional, educational, or business use. Please
contact your local bookseller or the Macmillan Corporate and Premium Sales Department
at (800) 221-7945 ext. 5442 or by email at MacmillanSpecialMarkets@macmillan.com.

FIRST
EDITION

First edition, 2021
Edited by Dave Roman
Cover and interior book design by Molly Johanson
Spiders consultant: Dr. Fiona Cross

Printed in China by Toppan Leefung Printing Ltd., Dongguan City, Guangdong Province

Penciled, inked, and colored digitally in Photoshop CC using a Wacom MobileStudio Pro
and a standard round Wacom pen nib.

Paperback: 10 9 8 7 6 5 4
Hardcover: 10 9 8 7 6 5 4 3 2

Spiders—they strike fear in some, fascination in others. Yell out "Spider!" in a room full of your friends and see what happens—half your friends will shriek in terror, and the other half will ask, "Where? Let me see it!"

When I was in college, I worked with researchers studying some gnarly trees growing on cliff faces, and while swinging from a climbing rope, I noticed that spiders were living a great life in the nooks and crannies of the cliffs. They were spinning big webs across sections of the rock and doing an amazing job of catching flies and other insects whizzing by. From that day on, I started to notice spiders everywhere, and I guarantee this will happen to you too! Our eight-legged friends are among the most common critters on the planet—they can be found living in forests or in washed-up seaweed on beaches, skating across small ponds while looking to catch fish, or even surviving on the slopes of Mount Everest. I've done my own research on Arctic spiders, and during the summer months in the far north, you can find wolf spiders every time you take a step—that's thousands of spiders per acre! In fact, arachnologists (the name for people who study spiders and their relatives) recently found that almost every home contains spiders, perhaps living in a dark closet or scurrying around the bathroom floor. I've done my own estimates too, and in most habitats, you are always within three feet of a spider. But don't be scared! Very few spider species can actually hurt us—their venom is most suited for catching smaller prey, often insects. In fact, in some croplands, spiders eat so many pest insects they actually help make sure farmers' fields are growing better food for us. They also eat insects that might hurt us or annoy us, such as mosquitoes. Some spiders eat other spiders too—taking over their web and devouring the resident.

Spiders are master weavers, but unlike Spider-Man (who uses high-tech webshooters attached to his wrists), spiders jet out their silken strands from specialized organs on their back ends. They use their threads to catch their prey, but they also use it to wrap up their eggs, or build protective shelters up in the corners of your bedroom or (as I learned!) on cliff faces. Some spiders can whip around a strand of silk (with a drop of glue at the end) and snag a moth—these are tiny little cowboys with silken lassos. Spiders also use silk to get airborne—they release threads upward, and their small bodies can be carried skyward, to be found thousands of feet in the air, before landing on isolated islands, perhaps in the middle of the Pacific Ocean. Even though we have known about this behavior for centuries, scientists are only now starting to understand how spiders do this "ballooning" (spoiler: it has to do with electrical currents!). Some spiders don't use silk to hunt; this includes spitting spiders, who hock a glue-like loogie at their prey.

And yet despite all the cool facts, some people are still scared of spiders, and a serious case of spider-fear is called "arachnophobia." Experts think such fear may be because we heard scary stories about spiders when we were children and it stuck with us. In some parts of the world, there are a few kinds of spiders that might bite humans and cause a reaction that may need a trip to the doctor, and arachnophobia may be an evolutionary adaptation rooted in these kinds of rare reactions. There's good news, though, because education is the gateway to turn fear into fascination, and the pages you are about to read will fill you with awe and wonder. You will learn about different kinds of spiders found around the world, and you will join Peter and Charlotte on a voyage of discovery, whether learning how silk is made, how spiders "balloon," or what amazing ways that spiders care for their young.

So, let's spin you a tale, and if you are a little worried, take a deep breath, open your mind, and be ready to learn about the planet's most incredible creatures. And the next time you are visiting a park, climbing around on some rocks, or waiting for a bus, keep your spidey sense on alert: an eight-legged friend is always close by, perhaps getting ready to sail the skies or catch a pest or two.

Professor Christopher Buddle
Arachnologist
McGill University, Montreal (Canada)

2

4

Since the beginning of language, people have categorized other living things. It has always been essential to know what kinds of plants you can eat and what kinds of animals might harm you!

But the modern scientific system of naming and defining groups of organisms by their physical traits is called taxonomy! Here's where I fit in the taxonomic ranking system!

KINGDOM: ANIMALIA

All animals on earth belong in this group! Most animals breathe oxygen, consume organic material, and can move around freely.

PHYLUM: EUARTHROPODA

Insects, arachnids, and crustaceans are all arthropods. They are invertebrates with an exoskeleton (which helps support their bodies and protect their organs), a segmented body, and pairs of jointed appendages.

CLASS: ARACHNIDA

All arachnids have eight legs, making them easy to distinguish from insects, which only have six. Besides spiders this class includes:

Scorpions

Ticks

Mites

Opiliones (or "harvestmen")

Solifuges (or "sunspiders," which aren't actually spiders!)

ORDER: ARANEAE

Spiders are the largest order of arachnids and one of the most diverse orders of all living organisms. They live on every continent except Antarctica and have colonized every environment except for the air and the open ocean!

FAMILY: THERIDIIDAE

Also known as cobweb or tangle-web spiders. Even though other parasteatoda species are mostly found in Asia, the resilient Theridiidae family can also be found across Europe and the Americas! In fact, it's the family you're most likely to encounter if you live in a home in North America!

GENUS: PARASTEATODA

A group made up of about 44 different species of mostly old-world spiders, meaning ones that originate in Europe, Asia, and Africa, as opposed to new-world spiders, which originate mostly in North or South America.

NEW WORLD

OLD WORLD

SPECIES: PARASTEATODA TEPIDARIORUM

FEMALE

MALE

That's me! This is the species anyone living in a home in North America is most likely to encounter. If you see cobwebs built in your attic or basement, they were probably built by one of these!

But it's also likely that the wide-spread fear is due in part to social conditioning! It can be learned by watching other people be afraid of spiders or even by seeing their depiction in media as monsters!

A study at Ohio State University showed that when seeing a live spider, people who have a fear of spiders are much more likely to overestimate its size than people without that fear!

Even modern medicine can have a bias against spiders! There are almost forty medical conditions, including skin cancer and several deadly skin infections, that are often misdiagnosed by doctors as brown recluse spider bites.

Black widows also have a reputation as a "deadly" species, but there were no deaths that resulted from the 2,246 reported black widow bites in the USA in 2016.

The truth is that of the 48,353 known species of spider, only 200 or so can cause serious injury to humans.

Some species are more territorial, but spiders will only bite humans if threatened, and they won't always inject a full dose or even any venom at all when making a defensive bite.

Long-Bodied Cellar Spider
Pholcus phalangioides
6–9 millimeters* (0.24–0.35 inch)
Often called "daddy long legs," but
not to be confused with harvestmen!

Isn't it true they're the
most venomous spiders on earth,
but their fangs aren't big enough
to pierce human skin?

Nope! Their venom
isn't much stronger
than any similarly
sized spider.

Gray Wall Jumper
Menemerus bivittatus
7–10 mm (0.27–0.39 in)
Very commonly found in man-made
structures, these spiders are especially
helpful to humans because they mainly prey
on mosquitoes, flies, and other pests!

BZZ

Golden Huntsman Spider
Olios giganteus
Females 19–21 mm (0.75–0.82 in)
Males 10–17 mm (0.39–0.67 in)
Huntsman spiders can grow to be larger than some other
house-dwelling spiders and may seem aggressive due to their
speed and agility, but their bite is not dangerous to humans.

*Sizes on these labels refer to the size of the spiders' bodies, but
including outstretched legs, it can be up to five times that number!

Black widows, like many web-weaving spiders, begin capturing prey by wrapping it in thick bands of silk, using their front legs to spin the prey rapidly and back legs to pull the silk. This process helps immobilize prey quickly!

WHO_OO_OA!!

Theridiidae spiders like the black widow are sometimes called comb-footed spiders because of a special row of bristles on their hind "feet" that help them spread silk quickly over prey.

For more dangerous prey, like wasps or crickets, the wrapping process only takes a second or two as the spider tries to avoid being bitten or stung! This speed also comes in handy when multiple victims are in the web at the same time!

Why I oughta!

What's up, bug-breath! You losers having your sewing circle?

Butt-rope weavin'— *AHH! HELP!*

Speaking of lunch!

Hey, no! Stay away from me!

To bite prey, the spider uses their fangs, which are part of its front appendages, called *chelicerae!* ("kuh-lis-er-ee")

The fangs are articulated and normally rest in a small groove in the chelicerae like the blade of a folding knife.

Serrated edge for cutting silk threads or mashing up food.

The opening to inject venom is just above the tip of the fang. This prevents clogging and makes the tip less likely to be damaged when biting into prey.

Most modern spiders fall into two distinct categories, partially based on the way their chelicerae move!

Araneomorphae

- 93–94% of modern spiders
- Usually smaller in size
- Shorter lifespan, 1–3 years
- Chelicerae move sideways

Mygalomorphae

- Usually larger: tarantulas, etc.
- Can live for up to 25 years
- Chelicerae move outward

The oldest spider ever recorded, an Australian trapdoor spider, lived to be 43!

TOOOOT

Chelicerae are also useful for things like digging or carrying eggs. The assassin spiders use their elongated chelicerae to spear prey!

Venom is pushed out by powerful muscles surrounding the venom glands, which lie either inside the chelicerae or extend deeper into the head and thorax, also known as the cephalothorax.

Brain

Venom Gland

Mouth Opening & Esophagus

Uurg...

Once the venom is injected, it takes effect quickly.

Spider venoms can contain neurotoxins, which affect the central nervous system and either immobilize or kill prey depending on the kind of venom and strength of the dose delivered.

They can also contain cytotoxins, which help break down the internal tissues and organs of their prey to make it more digestible.

Using a special sucking stomach, the spider sucks the liquefied innards out of the insect, filtering out anything too big to swallow with bristles surrounding their mouth.

YUM!

Adult spiders also have intestinal systems that allow them to go a long time without eating. A black widow can go months without food as long as it has water!

SLURP SLURP

BUG GULP

But we also get a lot of water from our food as well!

Yup! Butterflies, moths, bees, beetles, fleas, mites, crickets, and some ants make silk too, but usually only one kind during the larval stages of their life.

A spider, on the other hand, has appendages called spinnerets on their abdomen that allow them to make up to eight different types of silk.

Silkworms are the number one producer of silk used in fabric throughout the world! Their silk is very similar to spiders', but they produce large quantities all at once to build cocoons, which can be boiled to release the silk fibers.

But spider silk has a few advantages!

Its stickiness and elasticity could lead to stitches that help a wound close better.

Because of its strength, it could be used to make artificial muscles!

It's already being used to improve the effectiveness of car airbags and bulletproof vests!

Modern means of extracting spider silk are far from efficient though! It would take about a million spiders and a team of seventy people *two years* to produce a postcard-sized piece of fabric made from spider silk!

Silkworms mostly eat mulberry leaves, so keeping a lot of them together isn't a problem, but spiders, well...

They eat other spiders! This makes keeping large quantities of them for farming silk difficult!

Hey, cut it out!

CHOMP CHOMP

When researchers at the University of Wyoming tried to use a big group of spiders to produce silk for research, the territorial spiders either ate or killed one another.

But they realized that the solution was simple:

GOATS!

CHEW CHEW CHEW

Uh...goats?

Yup! GOATS!

Genetic modification is a process used to produce desired traits in plants or animals, and humans have been doing it for over ten thousand years. The most basic form of this is selective breeding—picking out "superior" individuals, which are used to breed offspring that inherit "superior" traits!

Plants grown for food could be modified over time by only planting seeds from the ones that were drought or flood resistant, tastier, or prettier.

Modern dogs and cats are the product of centuries of selective breeding!

Today there are more precise ways to genetically modify organisms! Using a process called transfection (transfer + infection), foreign DNA can be inserted into the nucleus of a cell! A few methods of doing this are:

Ouch!

OoOoH! Tingly!

Urrp, I think I'm gonna be sick...

Injecting DNA directly into the nucleus.

Electrocuting the cell to create holes in the cell wall or membrane.

Or using a virus that can't replicate itself to deliver foreign DNA into the host cell!

All these methods and more let us do some pretty amazing things to the germ line, or lineage of cells and DNA passed from parents to children!

This was exactly the tool that the researchers needed to produce larger amounts of spider silk in a much shorter period of time!

Wait, I thought they needed—

Goats? They needed both! By introducing some of the silk-producing genes of a golden orb-weaver into a goat embryo, they created goats that look and act like normal goats, but whose milk contains spider-silk proteins!

SPIDER MILK
SPIDER MILK

By separating the proteins from the milk, we can make spider silk faster and more efficiently than ever before!

HISSS

Whoa...

290 MILLION YEARS AGO: Oldest true spider fossil. mygalomorphs and araneomorphs make up 99.9% of all living spiders today, but the third group, Mesothelae, are the closest relatives to these first true spiders. These spiders had two or four spinnerets in the middle of their abdomen. They used their silk to line their burrows, which reinforced the walls and helped regulate the temperature within.

380 MILLION YEARS AGO: Oldest *Attercopus* fossil. *Attercopus fimbriunguis* is one of the spider's oldest relatives. Systematists, who classify organisms into taxonomical ranks by studying their evolution and relationships with other animals, originally classified it as the oldest spider ever, but later they realized its silk glands weren't true spinnerets.

305 MILLION YEARS AGO: Oldest *Idmonarachne* fossil. *Idmonarachne brasieri* is named after the father of Arachne in the Greek myth that gave arachnids their name! These spiderlike arthropods still had a segmented abdomen and still had no spinnerets, but it's easy to see how that segmented backside eventually became the smooth one spiders have today!

419 MILLION YEARS AGO: Oldest trigonotarbid fossil. Although they are more closely related to modern harvestmen than spiders, these early arachnids share a few distinct characteristics with modern spiders, like their eight legs and one pair of pedipalps, two-part body, and pocketknife-style fang-tipped chelicerae, although they had no venom glands.

24

A spinneret is a structure made up of multiple glands and spigots. Spiders can have up to seven different kinds of silk glands, each of which produces a unique silk. Here are the seven glands and spinnerets of a female golden silk orb-weaver.

Major & Minor Ampullate Glands
Major ampullate silk is the base for most webs. It's also used for the dragline, which many spiders leave behind them everywhere, allowing them to stop a fall or retreat to their burrow. Minor ampullate threads are used while building webs as well.

Piriform Glands
These glands produce tiny discs of sticky silk, which are used to glue threads in a web together to improve stability. They harden on contact with the air and can stick to a wide variety of materials. These discs also serve as the anchors for dragline threads!

Aggregate Glands*
Creates glue that coats flagelliform thread as it leaves the spinnerets. This makes the sticky silk that orb-weavers use to catch prey.

Aciniform Glands
The toughest of the silks! It can bend or deform without breaking, so it's perfect for wrapping prey!

Flagelliform Glands*
The "capture spiral" of a web is made of this extremely elastic silk. When something flies into the web, it can stretch far, giving the glue longer to stick to the insect.

**Only orb-weavers have these two glands!

Tubuliform Glands
Most modern female spiders make their egg sacs from this silk! This is the stiffest kind of silk, meaning it can withstand more direct force to better protect the eggs inside.

But when we make any of those silks, they're formed inside us as a liquid! It's the special shape of the spider's silk glands as well as their spinnerets that allow it to be formed into a solid thread!

Silk is mostly proteins, which are made up of long chains of amino acids. Under a powerful microscope, they look like a bunch of small coiled-up springs!

BOING   BOING

PANAPHONICS

BOING

Liquid proteins are stored in these glands until needed, when they are then forced rapidly through a thin duct with tight turns. This is where the magic happens!

The lining of this long structure removes some water from the liquid silk, and the thin squeeze orients the proteins into a long structured fiber. This realignment of proteins is what gives spider silk its strength and durability!

Move it!

Outta my way!

Each spigot has a valve that regulates the amount of silk leaving the gland or clamps down to stop us from falling.

SILK FIBER

VALVE MUSCLE

LIQUID SILK

Clusters of spigots make up each spinneret. The spigots make tiny strands of silk that fuse with the ones nearby, and the weight of the spider or the pulling motion of their foot extrudes the liquid silk into a solid thread!

27

Most spiders have six spinnerets laid out in three rows of two located on the end of their abdomen.

Mesothelae

Tarantula

Golden Silk Orb-Weaver

But they can have between two and eight! Orb-weavers tend to have more, as they produce a wider variety of silks.

They're movable too! Each spinneret has muscles surrounding it, which allow it to move in tandem with others or independently, giving the spider a lot of control when laying down silk.

Liphistiidae, the only living family of Mesothelae spiders, has the same spinnerets as its ancient relatives. These are located on the bottom side of their abdomen and are mostly used to line their burrows with silk.

Who would've thought so much was going on in that giant butt!

How *RUDE!*

Hold up. You said there were eight kinds of silk, but you only told us about seven of them!

HAH! No detail spared? I can answer this one!

Cribellate spiders have a special organ located above their spinnerets called a cribellum, made up of one or more plates covered in thousands of microscopic holes.

THIS THING!

These holes produce fine strands of silk that are brushed out by a special comb on their back feet called a calamistrum. This process results in a woolly silk that forms a powerful adhesive that doesn't dry out!

Fine, fine! I forgot one thing! I can't be expected to remember *every* detail of every old spider on earth, but I can teach you to build nature's most amazing achievement—

THE ORB WEB!

Why do they call it that?

Because the word "orb" used to also mean "ring" or "circle," and the name has stuck for hundreds of years!

HOW to MAKE

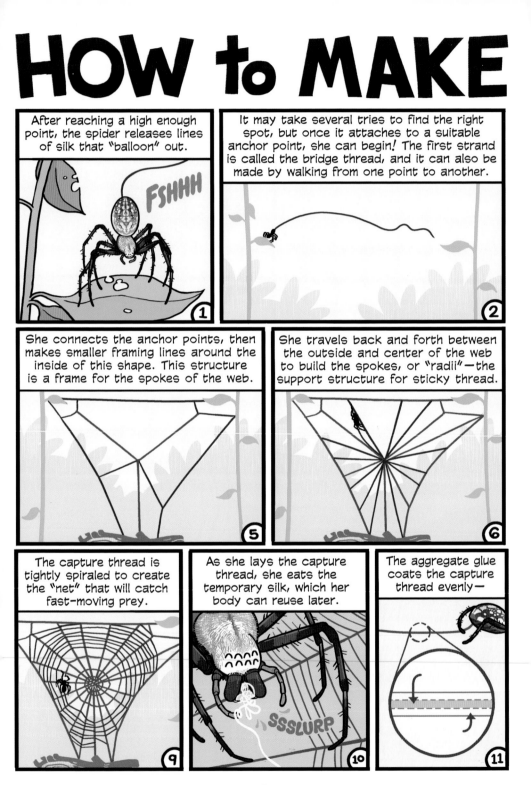

1. After reaching a high enough point, the spider releases lines of silk that "balloon" out.

FSHHH

2. It may take several tries to find the right spot, but once it attaches to a suitable anchor point, she can begin! The first strand is called the bridge thread, and it can also be made by walking from one point to another.

5. She connects the anchor points, then makes smaller framing lines around the inside of this shape. This structure is a frame for the spokes of the web.

6. She travels back and forth between the outside and center of the web to build the spokes, or "radii"—the support structure for sticky thread.

9. The capture thread is tightly spiraled to create the "net" that will catch fast-moving prey.

10. As she lays the capture thread, she eats the temporary silk, which her body can reuse later.

SSSLURP

11. The aggregate glue coats the capture thread evenly—

an ORB WEB!

She doubles back with a looser thread and then cuts the bridge thread in the middle by biting it.

CHOMP

3

She drops from the middle and anchors the looser thread to the ground, creating a **Y** shape that forms the base of the web.

4

The first spiral on the web is made with minor ampullate silk. This is temporary thread that is used to stabilize the web.

7

She releases flagelliform silk coated with aggregate glue. This forms the capture thread that prey sticks to.

THWIP

8

—so at the end of each section, she flicks the thread, breaking up the glue into smaller droplets, which will bond to prey much faster.

TWANG

12

And there you have it! Orb-weavers often hang head down in the center of the web, using vibrations to tell when prey has been caught.

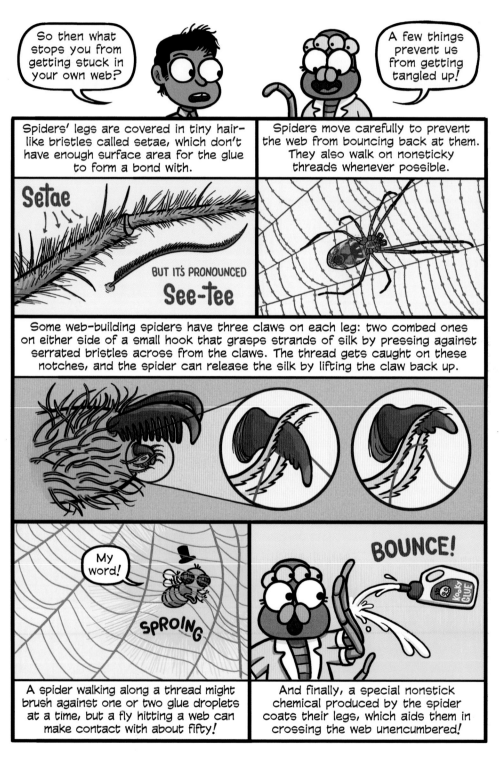

So then what stops you from getting stuck in your own web?

A few things prevent us from getting tangled up!

Spiders' legs are covered in tiny hair-like bristles called setae, which don't have enough surface area for the glue to form a bond with.

Setae

BUT IT'S PRONOUNCED
See-Tee

Spiders move carefully to prevent the web from bouncing back at them. They also walk on nonsticky threads whenever possible.

Some web-building spiders have three claws on each leg: two combed ones on either side of a small hook that grasps strands of silk by pressing against serrated bristles across from the claws. The thread gets caught on these notches, and the spider can release the silk by lifting the claw back up.

My word!

SPROING

BOUNCE!

Kooky GLUE

A spider walking along a thread might brush against one or two glue droplets at a time, but a fly hitting a web can make contact with about fifty!

And finally, a special nonstick chemical produced by the spider coats their legs, which aids them in crossing the web unencumbered!

32

But orb-weavers don't all build webs the exact same way either!

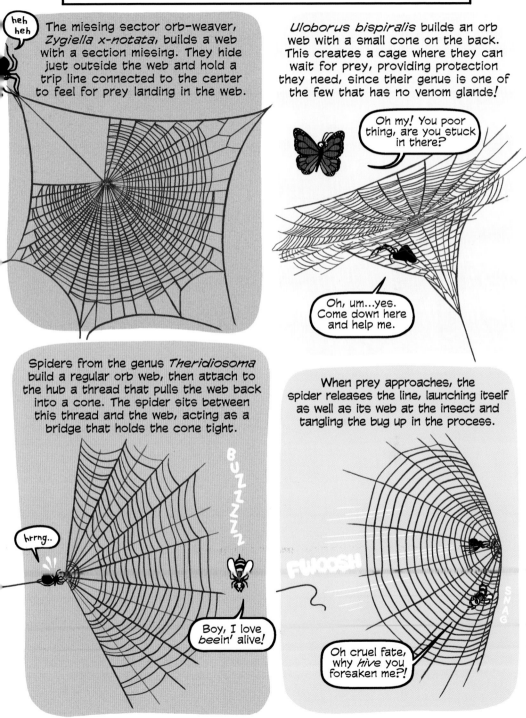

The missing sector orb-weaver, *Zygiella x-notata*, builds a web with a section missing. They hide just outside the web and hold a trip line connected to the center to feel for prey landing in the web.

heh heh

Uloborus bispiralis builds an orb web with a small cone on the back. This creates a cage where they can wait for prey, providing protection they need, since their genus is one of the few that has no venom glands!

Oh my! You poor thing, are you stuck in there?

Oh, um...yes. Come down here and help me.

Spiders from the genus *Theridiosoma* build a regular orb web, then attach to the hub a thread that pulls the web back into a cone. The spider sits between this thread and the web, acting as a bridge that holds the cone tight.

hrrng..

BUZZZZZ

Boy, I love beein' alive!

When prey approaches, the spider releases the line, launching itself as well as its web at the insect and tangling the bug up in the process.

FWOOSH

SNAG

Oh cruel fate, why *hive* you forsaken me?!

33

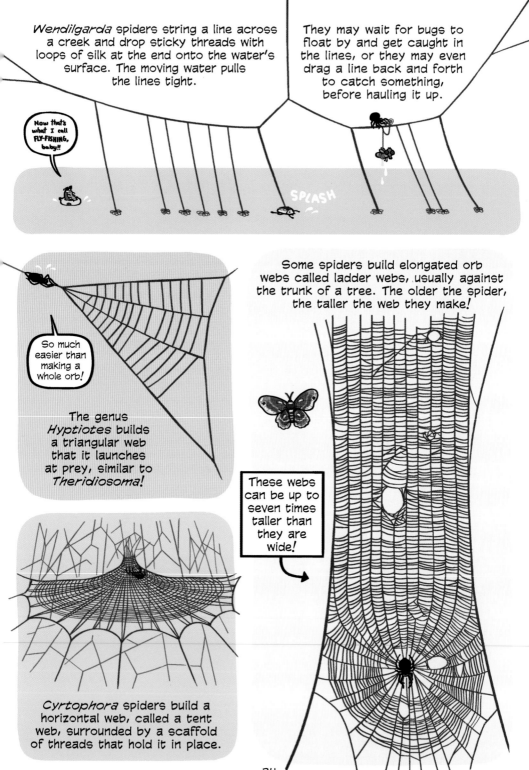

Wendilgarda spiders string a line across a creek and drop sticky threads with loops of silk at the end onto the water's surface. The moving water pulls the lines tight.

They may wait for bugs to float by and get caught in the lines, or they may even drag a line back and forth to catch something, before hauling it up.

Now that's what I call FLY-FISHING, baby!!

SPLASH

So much easier than making a whole orb!

The genus *Hyptiotes* builds a triangular web that it launches at prey, similar to *Theridiosoma*!

Cyrtophora spiders build a horizontal web, called a tent web, surrounded by a scaffold of threads that hold it in place.

Some spiders build elongated orb webs called ladder webs, usually against the trunk of a tree. The older the spider, the taller the web they make!

These webs can be up to seven times taller than they are wide!

*Scent intended to attract potential mates

Elegant Crab Spider
Xysticus elegans
Females 8-10 mm (0.3-0.39 in)
Males 6-7 mm (0.24-0.28 in)
Crab spider generally refers to
members of the family Thomisidae,
but the ones who use flowers to
hunt are called flower crab spiders!

Pink Crab Spider
Thomisus onustus
Females 6-7 mm (0.24-0.28 in)
Males 2-4 mm (0.08-0.16 in)
Other colors include white or yellow.
Most crab spiders are ambush hunters!
They use their natural camouflage to
blend in with leaves, bark, or in this case,
flowers, and they can wait motionless for
long periods of time—for unsuspecting
prey to get close enough—before quickly
pinning and biting their prey to deliver a
dose of very powerful venom.

It seems like lots
of spiders spend most
of their time not really
moving at all.

Northern Crab Spider
Mecaphesa asperata
Females 4–6 mm (0.16–0.24 in)
Males 3–4 mm (0.12–0.16 in)
Crab spider venom liquefies their victims' innards, which are sucked out through the bite holes. This usually leaves the exoskeleton of the dead bug completely intact!

White-Banded Crab Spider
Misumenoides formosipes
Female 5–11 mm (0.20–0.43 in)
Males 2–4 mm (0.08–0.16 in)
May also be yellow, brown, or light blue. Most likely called crab spiders because their front pairs of legs can be more than twice as long as their back pairs and are powerful enough to pin down bees, wasps, and butterflies without help from silk wrapping!

It takes a lot of work to build a web or grapple with a bug, so we like to use our energy efficiently in between meals, otherwise we can run out of silk or even die!

Plus, a spider moving around in a web or on a flower is a lot easier for predators or prey to spot, so we're more likely to eat and less likely to get eaten if we stay still!

Misumena vatia, the goldenrod crab spider, can even change color to suit the kind of flower they're on! They hunt on a wide variety of flowers that are varying shades of yellow and white, like daisies and sunflowers.

It can take anywhere between a week to a month to change from yellow to white.

Hurry up already!

Slowly, the pigments on its outer layer of cells change to mimic its habitat.

It's possible this is a natural form of crypsis—which means an ability used to avoid detection from potential predators or prey! But it's also possible that they change their color in relation to the amount of sunlight they're receiving as a form of shielding against UV radiation!

Whoa, so it's like sunscreen that their body makes whenever it needs to? I guess that makes sense if they're hanging out on top of flowers in the sun all day.

Hey—I've noticed something. It seems like in most spider species the males are a lot smaller than the females. Why is that?

Most spiders exhibit sexual dimorphism, which means that males and females have different physical traits from each other! There are lots of animals that are sexually dimorphic aside from spiders too!

Size dimorphism is one of the most common ways in which spiders differ, as the females of most species are much larger than the males. Female *Argiope aemula* can be more than ten times the size of their male counterparts!

Coloration and body shape is another way to tell males and females apart!

Grey Wall Jumper males and females are the same size but have different patterns on their back.

Spiny-Backed Orb-Weaver males lack red spikes around their abdomen.

Male spiders mature faster too! To grow larger, young spiders molt often.

Beneath their exoskeleton, they grow a larger one, which is softer and folded.

They suspend themselves upside down and shed their old exoskeleton by pushing against it until it cracks.

POP

Then, they slowly wriggle their way free and let their new exoskeleton unfold and harden.

At last! Free from this prison of flesh!

Males are often smaller, so they need fewer molts to become fully mature and reproduce. After his final molt, he abandons web building or even hunting until he finds a female to mate with.

gone matin'

Whereas females' pedipalps resemble a short pair of legs, during their last molt, males gain a special bulb on each palp that is used in fertilization.

FEMALE   MALE

But before that, he needs to find a female to court! Locating a female that is mature and willing to mate can be difficult.

WEB of LOVE
MATCH NOW

But females secrete pheromones—chemicals that trigger a social or physical response in members of the same species—to attract males. Some leave pheromones on their web or dragline to guide males to them!

When a spider comes across a pheromone web, he eats or destroys it before it can attract other males. Reproduction is the main drive for a mature male, so competition is fierce!

46

But other guys are the least of his concerns. A female may not be that picky about which things in her web get eaten! Males may wait until a female has fed before trying to mate so that they don't become the meal!

Nooo! I only wanted love!

And it's not just hunger—spiders of all kinds may eat a potential suitor just because they don't want to mate with him! This means spiders have developed some elaborate courtship rituals. This behavior also helps spiders recognize one another as members of the same species when pheromones aren't enough!

Some male nursery web spiders will catch a fly, wrap it in silk, and bring it to a female as a gift so that she might be less interested in eating him.

TWANG TWANG

A male orb-weaver may attach a thread to a female's web that he plucks rhythmically. Sound and vibration are two important parts of many spiders' courtship rituals!

DUM DUM DUM DUM DUM DUM

Some jumping spiders perform complex dances by raising and lowering their abdomen and drumming on the ground.

SHAKE SHAKE

SHAKE SHAKE

Maratus volans, the peacock spider, has special flaps on his back. When lifted up, they form a colorful plumage! He waves this along with his legs to court a mate.

Since a male spider's main instinct is to reproduce, he may try several times before running out of energy and dying.

R.I.P.
DIDN'T DO ANYTHING. DIED.

But he may only get one chance! The females of some species, like *Araneus pallidus*, often begin eating the male partway through mating!

CRUNCH

Neat! Isn't that where black widows get their name? I heard they always eat the males as well!

No, that's just their bad reputation! Male black widows usually get away unharmed after mating.

Like most spider species, the male does have a chance of being eaten no matter what, but some *Latrodectus* species even share their web and catch prey with the male for a week or two after mating!

After mating, it takes a few weeks before the female is ready to lay eggs. Most are only about 1 mm (0.04 in) wide, but the number of spiderlings different species give birth to can vary widely!

Araneus spiders lay about 1,000 eggs in around ten minutes. A spider's heart rate triples while laying eggs!

But *Cupiennius* have them beat: they can lay up to 2,500 eggs in eight minutes!

Most spiders lay large broods of eggs, but not all! *Oonops* species lay only 2 eggs at a time!

And the tiny *Monoblemma* spiders lay only 1 large egg at a time!

Once the eggs are laid, the spider builds a cocoon of silk around them to protect them from harsh environments or egg eaters like wasps and flies. It also acts as insulation against dangerous temperatures!

The long-bodied cellar spider ties its eggs in a few strands of silk and then carries her egg sac around in her chelicerae until they hatch!

But most egg casings are much more complex! Many spiders, like *Araneus quadratus*, begin by laying out a thin silk disc built up of tightly woven threads.

They climb onto the bottom of the disc and begin laying silk around the edges of it, which slowly builds up into a chamber where they lay the eggs. This process takes about two hours.

Once the eggs are laid, she holds them in with a fine layer of silk and then surrounds the eggs with a thick liquid that hardens and cements them all together.

The spider then covers the structure with a loose thread that she layers up in a mesh pattern. This becomes the hard shell surrounding the entire egg chamber.

I hope we stay this close forever!

This outer shell may harden or be tightly wound enough that the threads merge.

But there are a lot of ways to wrap our eggs. Let's start with my species!

American House Spider
Parasteatoda tepidariorum
Resembles a tiny brown paper bag, but **DO NOT** pack your lunch in it. Trust me on this one.

Grass Spider
Agelenopsis pennsylvanica
A thin contact-lens-shaped web attaches the eggs to leaves or bark. Bad substitute for a normal contact lens unless you like looking at spiders.

Basilica Orb-Weaver
Mecynogea lemniscata
Multiple egg sacs stuck together with web, like a string of pearls filled with baby spiders!

Yellow Garden Spider
A tough papery shell that looks like a pear but tastes like your worst nightmares.

Silver Garden Spider
Argiope argentata
A flat blob that, let's be honest with each other, looks a lot like a booger.

Brown Widow
Latrodectus geometricus
Looks like a fuzzy little explosion, more so when the spiders pop out.

Silkhenge Spider
These incredible egg sacs found in the Amazon are built by a spider that is still unknown to arachnologists! No joke!

Agroeca brunnea creates a small paper-lantern-like structure that includes a molting chamber for the emerging spiderlings to spread into immediately after hatching.

MOLTING CHAMBER

Some spiders—like the jumping spider, *Marpissa rumpfi*—build a nest of layered silk and eggs attached to the ceiling of their burrow.

And wolf spiders, members of the family Lycosidae, build very tough round egg casings!

Wolf spiders? Yeah, I think this is where the tour ends for me.

But because they hunt on the go and often don't build webs, they prefer to carry egg sacs around on their back by attaching them to their spinnerets!

In most cases, when the spiderlings are ready to hatch, they use digestive secretions to dissolve the inside layer of web and then gradually push aside the tougher outer fibers to make an opening.

Nursery web spiders carry their eggs in their chelicerae until just before the eggs hatch. They then build a tentlike web and hang the egg sac inside of it. The spiderlings stay in the web for a few days once they hatch.

Hey, kids! Dinnertime!

BARF

About twenty species of spiders provide food for their offspring by catching prey for them, regurgitating already liquefied food, or even by laying a batch of unfertilized eggs for the young ones to eat!

Some spiders sacrifice themselves to feed their kids! Matriphagy, or "mom eating," occurs in a few spiders, such as *Cheiracanthium japonicum*, who allow their young to eat them alive, helping them gain weight quicker and giving them a better chance of survival.

YES, EAT OF MY FLESH THAT YOU MAY LIVE!

CHEW
CHEW
CHEW
CHEW
CHEW
CHEW
CHEW
CHEW
CHEW

Num num, sorry, mommy!

Even more bizarrely, the crab spider *Australomisidia ergandros* converts nutrients from food into hemolymph—the spider equivalent of blood—which is then sucked out through bites in the mother's legs until she is unable to move and is finally devoured fully.

Hey, do you think Mom would do that for us?

Ewww, shut up!

Spiders are great at fishing too! There are species from a few families that specialize in hunting on or *in* water!

Is nowhere safe?!

The majority of spiders will drown in a pool or river, but some species have a covering of water-repellant hairs called a hydrophobic cuticle, which keeps them dry, even when they're fully submerged in water!

WATER

TRAPPED AIR

Some water spiders use the wind to sail across the surface of the water.

Others row across the surface with their legs.

When attacking prey, some can even gallop across the top of the water at five times their normal speed!

But the water is a dangerous place too! Spiders in open water can make a quick meal for a passing fish or frog.

Oh, here we go! This is a great spot to see some fishing spiders in action!

Long-Jawed Orb-Weaver
Tetragnatha extensa
Females 10-12 mm (0.39-0.47 in)
Males 7-9 mm (0.28-0.35 in)
Although these orb-weavers don't
necessarily use water to hunt, they
do prefer to build webs in marshy
or watery areas and are faster at
running on water than they are on land!

Salt-Marsh Wolf Spider
Pardosa purbeckensis
Females 6-7 mm (0.24-0.28 in)
Males 5-6 mm (0.20-0.24 in)
Most wolf spiders have a thick
hydrophobic cuticle that aids them in
traveling around or on water.

Raft Spider
Dolomedes fimbriatus
Females 9-22 mm (0.35-0.87 in)
Males 9-15 mm (0.35-0.59 in)
Many water-dwelling species have white
stripes along the sides of their abdomen,
which help them blend in with reflections on
the surface of the water. They may dive
underwater to hunt or escape predators!

BLAAA

LAST ONE IN IS A ROTTEN SPIDER EGG!

SPLOOSH

Hey, what's that belt thingy?

Another one of my inventions! It lets me breathe while I'm underwater!

See, spiders don't breathe through our mouths! Small slits on the underside of our abdomen lead to organs called book lungs. These alternating hollow stacks of tissue allow us to filter oxygen out of the air!

Hemolymph, the spider equivalent of blood, passes through alternating stacks and absorbs oxygen to be transported to the spider's other organs and tissues.

X-RAY

WHY ARE THEY CALLED BOOK LUNGS?

HEMOLYMPH

AIR & OXYGEN

In addition to book lungs, or sometimes instead of them, spiders may have trachea that branch throughout their body. Spiders with a tracheal system (usually smaller, modern spiders) are better at retaining water and less prone to dehydration!

HEART

BOOK LUNG

TRACHEA

Book lungs may have actually evolved from fish gills, as the structure of the two are similar!

WATER

Spiders have what is called an open circulatory system, which means that hemolymph is pumped into the body cavity of the spider by its heart.

I'm just a big bag of blood!

This cavity, the hemocoel, is filled with passageways that hemolymph travels through as it washes over the internal organs to provide them with oxygen.

Oh good, it looks like he's home!

This is my friend the diving bell spider, *Argyroneta aquatica!*

Tepi! Hi, y'all! Wow, it's not often that I get this many visitors at once!

A diving bell starts with a sheet web, but as we add layers, we also like to spice this baby up a li'l bit!

RUB RUB RUB

We fill the spaces between the threads with a unique protein-rich hydrogel. This creates the outer layer of the bell that allows air to be trapped inside.

We form the bubble we live in by transporting air on our backs from the surface and brushing it off to get trapped underneath the web. Hydrogels behave similarly to tissue like skin in that they are absorbent and made up of mostly water!

FWISH FWISH

OXYGEN

CO2

Because of this, *gas exchange* can take place between the bubble and the water outside. Animals are performing gas exchange when they breathe! Their cells take in oxygen and give off carbon dioxide, and the lungs pump those gases in and out of the body.

Both gases in the bubble exert different amounts of pressure on it, so when the spider breathes in or out it forces the bubble to equalize the pressure by removing or adding gas! The water contains more oxygen than the air in the bubble, so oxygen flows through the hydrogel and replenishes the air inside, while carbon dioxide the spider exhales flows out!

WATER

HYDROGEL

AIR

This means that about 70% of the air we breathe is recycled from the water around us! However, nitrogen does slowly diffuse out of the bubble without being replenished, so once a day, we need to bring air down from the surface, or the bubble will gradually disappear.

Ooh, speaking of which, mine could use some replenishing. I assume you're heading wherever Max was going?

You saw Maxie? When was this?!

WHERE?!

WHAT DID THEY SAY?!

Hey, calm down! I didn't talk to them, but they looked fine! It was half an hour ago. They were dragging leaves around up there.

OOOOH, they're heading right into the woods! We'd better go catch up to them. That forest is full of predators!

About 99% of spiders have eight eyes arranged in two or three rows on the front of their face. Each set of eyes has a name to help when comparing spiders! We break them up into four groups to describe which set we're talking about!

Posterior Median Eyes (PME)

Posterior Lateral Eyes (PLE)

Anterior Median Eyes (AME)

Anterior Lateral Eyes (ALE)

PLE PME PME PLE

ALE AME AME ALE

The AME are a spider's primary set of eyes. They usually appear black, since they lack an organ called a tapetum.

But this reflective surface in the inner eye is present in all of their secondary eyes. It can make these eyes appear to be different colors because they're so reflective!

Cornea

Lens

Retina

Optic Nerve

Tapetum

ANTERIOR MEDIAN EYES   SECONDARY EYES

Their reflectiveness also makes them more sensitive to light. In wolf spiders, the PME and PLE contain 15–35 times the light-sensitive cells of the AME!

Eye arrangement is helpful for arachnologists and arachnophiles to identify unknown species because many within a family or genus share similar faces!

Ant-Mimic Crab Spider
Amyciaea lineatipes

Wolf Spider
Alopecosa fabrilis

Magnolia Green Jumper
Lyssomanes viridis

Mangrove Jumper
Ligurra latidens

Goldenrod Crab Spider
Misumena vatia

Trap-Jaw Spider
Chilarchaea quellon

Southern Black Widow
Latrodectus mactans

Trapdoor Spider
Liphistius desultor

Wood-Louse Hunter
Dysdera crocata

Brown Recluse
Loxosceles reclusa

Malagasy Green Lynx Spider
Peucetia madagascariensis

Cobalt Blue Tarantula
Cyriopagopus lividus

Most members of the cribellate spider family Caponiidae have two eyes, but a few members of their family have four, six, or eight as well!

And a few species have no eyes at all! The eyeless huntsman spider, *Sinopoda scurion*, doesn't need them, since it lives deep in caves where there's no light at all! It relies entirely on its other sensory organs to hunt and survive.

And don't forget jumping spiders! These big-eyed babies are the largest spider family by far, making up 13% of all spiders in the world!

Yes! My favorite! No offense, Tepi...

None taken!

Those gorgeous colors! Those furry li'l palps! Those big ol' eyes!

THEY ARE THE CUTEST SPID—

doo dee doo

AHHH!

WOOSH

EEK!

Ah! Pardon me, I had no intention of frightening you!

Zebra Jumper
Salticus scenicus
Females 5-9 mm (0.20-0.35 in)
Males 5-6 mm (0.20-0.24 in)

Ohhhh! Even their labels are cute!

CRUNCH CRUNCH

JUST LOOK AT THOSE EYES! Tepi! Get me the shrink ray and set it on reverse. I'm taking a sweet furry angel home with me!

Ahem, excuse me, madam, but my eyes are *HIGHLY* evolved organs!

Jumping spiders' AME have highly developed retinas. The eye is elongated with many extra layers of cells called photoreceptors.

that's these things

These cells respond to light and send visual signals to our brains, which interpret what we see!

bzzzzz..

They spot prey with the other sets of eyes, which are better at detecting movement, and then quickly orient themselves toward their prey to focus with their AME before jumping.

They're much better for spotting prey than say, an orb-weaver's! Some spiders have fine vision at close range, but ours is better at spotting prey that's farther away!

And they're so cuuute!

Stop that!

Spiders without big adorable baby eyes still have several other powerful senses!

Some of the longer hairs that cover a spider's body contain sensitive nerves that allow them to sense touch and vibrations on the ground.

DOINK

Hey, quit pokin' me!

Although their legs and bodies are covered in thousands of these hairs, touching just one is enough to trigger a fight-or-flight response!

We also have specialized hairs in lines along our legs called trichobothria! These amazing organs can sense even the tiniest vibrations in the air and are specifically tuned to pick up the vibrations of insect wings beating.

Cupiennius spiders can detect a fly that's 30 centimeters (11.81 in) away, from just the vibration of its wings!

Spiders also have small slits covering their bodies and legs that sense bends and pressure on their exoskeleton.

This is vital because their outer layer is a hard shell that can't be deformed past a certain point without breaking!

They also sense vibration! Pirate spiders use them to locate prey struggling in the water nearby!

Yarr! Avast!

SPLISH SPLASH

Spiders also "taste" with their legs and palps using specialized hairs. They can tell the difference between a rotting and freshly dead bug and identify harmful chemicals or poisons they should avoid.

Eww! Who left this in here?!

Hey, make yourself useful! Jump up real high and look for a spider kid around here!

Fine, if you promise to leave me alone forever.

When jumping spiders take off, they are traveling at about 85 cm per second (1.9 miles per hour) and they can go up to 16 cm (6.3 in) in the air. For a human, that would be like jumping to the top of a nine-story building!

They're behind you.

SHIFF

One and three touch the ground while two and four are lifted off the ground and vice versa!

When the spider wants to turn, it takes longer strides on either the left or right side, causing it to move in the opposite direction!

This is why spiders curl up into a ball when they die: as their heart slows, they lose blood pressure and aren't able to push their legs out. A dehydrated spider may go through this same process!

Alas! I am no more!

Spiders also have an incredible defense mechanism built into their legs! When threatened or trapped, they can detach a leg at will to escape!

So long, dingus!

Shedding a piece of the body when threatened is called *autotomy!* This defense mechanism is shared by some other animals, like lizards, crabs, and even mice!

It isn't even necessary for a predator to be pulling on the limb for it to come off! And it's totally up to the spider when the leg goes. Spiders under anesthesia aren't able to perform this process!

POP

When the leg is fully detached, the muscles surrounding the joint close naturally to prevent a fatal loss of blood pressure. But as long as the spider hasn't gone through its final molt yet, it doesn't need to worry!

That's because spiders can actually regenerate their lost limbs!

If they lose a limb in the first half of the period between molts, it will start to grow back slowly!

This leg grows curled up inside the stump of the old leg, so it may grow to be thinner or smaller than the others.

BEFORE MOLTING

AFTER MOLTING

AFTER LAST MOLT

Is this the fastest a spider can go?

Nope, the fastest spider is the giant house spider, *Eratigena atrica*, who moves at almost 1.9 kilometers per hour (1.2 mph)!

FWOOOOOOSH

But some spiders forgo walking for more interesting transportation methods!

BOING

Wheeee!

The Moroccan flic-flac spider, *Cebrennus rechenbergi*, does leaping aerial front flips to escape from predators.

The wheel spider, *Carparachne aureoflava*, rolls down sand dunes on its side by curling its legs and flexing its joints to propel itself!

Hey, *uh*, how are we gonna stop when we need to?

The dragline acts as an anchor, so a spider just clamps down its spinnerets to come to a quick stop!

MAX'S BOAT!

Hey, you can stop now! You've proved you're the fastest!

Some spiders are *diurnal*: they hunt and build webs during the day. Others are nocturnal, or active at night! This one is a night hunter with a specialized silk that helps it quickly subdue prey.

Spitting Spider
Scytodes thoracica
Female 4–6 mm (0.16–0.24 in)
Male 3–4 mm (0.12–0.16 in)
These long-range hunters unleash a specialized silk from their cheliceral opening. This silk comes from their venom glands, making a potent mix of both silk proteins and venom!

It spits envenomed sticky silk in a zigzag, covering its prey in less than one seven-hundredth of a second.

FSSSH

The silk immobilizes the prey so that the spider can move in and wrap it with regular silk before delivering a fatal bite.

riiip

They're also *scavengers*: they'll happily eat a dead insect or other animal if they come across it.

If spider eyes are so bad, how do they see at night?

Our vision is terrible, but our eyes are highly light sensitive!

Spiders' sleeping and eating cycles are mostly determined by the time of day due to the changes in available light.

Ahh, another beautiful day for eating bugs!

Do you remember the reflective layer in some spiders' eyes—the tapetum? At night, it reflects light off the back of the eye, increasing the amount of light the eye can use, similar to the way night-vision goggles work!

This makes it easy to locate some species, like wolf spiders, at night! If you hold a flashlight level with your eyes and point it into a field, you may see one or several pairs of tiny green eyes flashing back at you!

That's probably a wolf spider! Holding the light at eye level will reflect it right back at your face. Otherwise, it's easy to miss!

Ogre-face spiders, members of the genus *Deinopis*, have night vision that is twice as powerful as a cat's or owl's!

Although these spiders have eight eyes, their PME are extremely enlarged and face forward, making them look particularly menacing. These spiders' eyes lack tapeta. Instead, they produce a super-light-sensitive membrane every single night that breaks down in the morning!

GRRR!

These cribellate spiders hold a small web between their front two pairs of legs, held straight out as they hang vertically off the ground. They spot prey with their powerful eyes and drop the net on it as it passes by.

BZZZZZZ

They remain motionless while hanging vertically, camouflaging themselves against the branches of the trees where they live!

Oh! Look over there!

California Trapdoor Spider
Bothriocyrtum californicum
20–32 mm (0.79–1.26 in)

Quelle surprise!

Trapdoor spiders live in silk-lined underground burrows. After the burrow has been dug, they make a silk disc, which they cover with dirt and dry brush.

The disc is attached with thick hinges of silk, making the trapdoor that covers the entrance to their home. They grip the inside with their chelicerae to keep it shut.

Some lay lines of silk leading out from their burrows and wait for the vibrations of an insect passing across them.

Some will jump out and chase down passing prey.

zoooooom

Some barely leave their burrow at all, only attacking things within easy reach.

yoink!

This helps protect them from other predators as well! Although many kinds of spiders also live in a burrow, the trapdoor is a unique advantage for this family of spiders.

Some trapdoor spiders, such as *Cyclocosmia* and *Galeosoma*, **are** the trapdoor! These spiders have a distinct abdomen with an intricate "seal" on the bottom that provides camouflage in soil.

When threatened, they retreat headfirst into their burrow, where their tapered, flat back creates a plug that prevents predators from getting to their softer bits!

Wouldn't living in a hole in the ground get lonely? Spiders are so solitary!

There's a small group, called social spiders, who spend loads of time together!

"Social spiders" isn't a group like "wolf spiders"—which is the informal term used to describe members of the family Lycosidae. Social spiders are what we call any species that cooperates in prey capture and/or brood care.

Velvet spiders, members of the family Eresidae

The huntsman spider *Delena cancerides*

Lynx spiders from the genus *Tapinillus*

Communal hunting is one of the great advantages social spiders have over others, as multiple spiders can work to take down larger prey than one spider could on their own. A bug caught in the communal web of *Anelosimus eximius* is shared by the whole group, meaning that any individual spider in the colony can go longer without catching prey and still survive.

Whoa! There are a lot of you here. Are we having a party or something?

The colony also provides a wider selection of mating partners, help caring for spiderlings, and better defense against predators!

Anelosimus eximius also builds some of the largest webs in the world! Communal webs can reach lengths of 7.62 meters (25 feet) and may contain upward of fifty thousand spiders. These huge webs can blanket whole trees or even forests when colonies join together.

Oh no, I think this is all my fault...

What do you mean?

Okay, this *has* to be the tree.

Max. I know why they came to *this* tree...

It's an ant colony! I've been researching ant mimics, spiders who have mastered the art of disguise! Max must've come to do research!

We'd better put on some disguises if we're going to try to enter an ant colony! Those things do *not* like outsiders!

Disguises?

That's right! And we'll make them ourselves.

Ants have been a viable food source for about sixty million years, and a variety of spiders have evolved over that time to better hunt them by copying their appearance, behavior, and even the chemicals they secrete!

Their body may be constricted, making it appear that they have three body segments, like an ant, and their legs are thinner than usual.

Some have enlarged spots on their head that look like an ant's eyes, and their enlarged chelicerae mimic an ant carrying something in its mandibles!

Okay, let's see your best ant faces!

Wow, we look absolutely terrible.

Yeah, I don't know if I'm gonna fool any ants with this disguise.

Ant

Oh, don't worry, here's the most important part!

ANT PHEROMONES QUEEN SIZE

FSSSH

≹COUGH COUGH≹

≹COUGH≹

Sorry, but it's necessary! Ants leave a trail of pheromones wherever they go, for other ants to follow, so you need to be dripping with this stuff.

ƧHACKƧ

spritz

spritz

When we join the line of ants, try to act like one of them, and don't sweat! It'll wash the pheromone right off you!

Uh... I'll try?

To blend in, spiders have to move like ants too. They can walk on their back three pairs of legs while holding up their front pair to mimic an ant's antennae!

They also move their abdomen up and down as they walk, like an ant does, making it easier to move about inside a colony without alerting the ants to their presence.

wiggle wiggle

Mimicry helps spiders stay alive too! Ants are a lot less palatable than a nice juicy spider, plus attacking an ant means a predator may have to deal with the whole colony, so blending in may save a spider from becoming the next meal!

In 1901, a scientist named Nikola Tesla began building an enormous device on Long Island in New York. Wardenclyffe Tower, as it was called, was conceived of as an experimental wireless-message transmission station.

But he soon theorized it could also transmit power wirelessly! He knew that the sun's upper atmosphere constantly releases solar wind—a stream of protons, electrons, and other electrically charged particles.

This stream passes continuously over the earth, so many of the particles accumulate in our atmosphere. The negative charge of the earth attracts the positive charge in the atmosphere, leading to a higher density of particles and a higher electrical charge closer to the earth's surface!

Tesla thought this meant he could turn the entire earth into a conductor and wirelessly transmit power to homes and factories worldwide. He was never able to test this, as all of his investors pulled out before the tower was completed.

Can I have two million dollars so I can give free electricity to everyone on earth forever?

Ummm... No.

NIKY'S FREE ELECTRICITY TOWER

BIG BUCK'S POWER CO.

BUCK

But what Tesla didn't know was that spiders had already harnessed that same electrical field millions of years ago to conquer the planet.

95

A study done in a windless chamber showed that spiders are still able to balloon if the chamber is charged with a mild electrical field. It also showed that their trichobothria hairs are *electroreceptive*, meaning they can detect changes in electrical fields!

Whee!

POWER LOAD

Part of why webs are so good at capturing insects is because spider silk usually carries a negative charge. When a positively charged insect hits the web, static electricity pulls the silk toward the bug!

This positively sucks!

Don't be so negative!

Before ballooning, a spider finds the highest point possible and prepares by sticking its abdomen in the air and standing on its claws, decreasing the amount of contact with the ground.

When it detects a powerful enough positive charge in the air with its trichobothria, it releases a few threads of negatively charged silk.

THWIP

FWOOSH

If the charge in the air is powerful enough, the "kite" gets pulled off the ground, and the spider along with it!

It's been our key to surviving all these years because it allows us to pick up and move when an environment no longer sustains us! Mass migrations are common, as particularly powerful electrical currents can induce large groups of us to all take to the air at once!

Spiders are a huge component of what we call aeroplankton—the trillions of tiny creatures traveling high in the air at all times. Spiders have been found up to 4 km (2.5 miles) in the air and more than 1,500 km (1,000 miles) out at sea!

They call it aeroplankton, but you know what I like to call it?

THE WORLD-WIDE WEB!

grooan

So where are we right now, exactly?

Well, the downside to being at the whim of the earth's electrical forces is you don't really get to choose where you go.

Edible Spider
Cyriopagopus albostriatus
These tarantulas are a local delicacy in parts of Cambodia, where they are called a-ping!

Elegant Golden Jumping Spider
Chrysilla lauta
These rainbow-colored spiders can be found in a variety of tropical places around the world.

Curved Spiny Spider
Macracantha arcuata
These li'l devils are found across the globe and probably got around by hiding in produce shipments!

Long-Jawed Orb-Weaver
Opadometa sarawakensis
The females of this species are brightly colored, but like many spiders, the males are duller and more earth-toned.

St. Andrew's Cross Spider
Argiope aetherea
The common name for these spiders is also used for many Argiope species, who build webs with an X-shaped stabilimentum.

Looks like we're over Southeast Asia, a region of the world partially made up of many small islands! Islands are usually isolated environments that have limited predators for any given species. This means more opportunities for unique spiders to evolve!

Spiny Orb-Weaver
Gasteracantha sacerdotalis
Spiny orb-weavers can be found across the globe with a variety of markings and brilliant colors!

Drag Tail Spider
Arachnura melanura
This spider uses its unique body shape to hide among dead leaves and branches!

Eight-Spotted Crab Spider
Platythomisus octomaculatus
This crab spider uses its black and yellow camouflage to hunt bees on the tops of flowers!

Tricolor Orb-Weaver
Cyrtarachne tricolor
These small web weavers can be found on other nearby islands as well!

Hey, soooo now seems like a good time to tell us what to do if we get bitten.

Oh right! Well, first, avoid bugging spiders at all!

Not every spider's venom will make you sick, but that doesn't mean you shouldn't be careful around them, especially if you don't know what kind of spider it is!

The first thing to do if you get bitten is tell an adult! For most bites, cleaning the wound with soap and water and using an antibiotic ointment is enough. Ice can help reduce swelling and pain.

But if the bite causes extreme or lasting pain, muscle cramps, fever, nausea, or loss of breath OR if you think the bite might be from a dangerous spider, you should seek medical help immediately!

Fortunately, for almost every dangerous spider on the planet, humans have made an antivenom! A tiny bit of a specific kind of venom is injected into an animal like a sheep or goat, and their immune system creates antibodies to fight it.

Now hold on just a sec...

These antibodies are most of what makes up an antivenom. They bond with the toxic venom components in your body and neutralize them.

ANTIBODY

This system is so effective that there have been no fatal bites from Sydney funnel-web spiders since their antivenom was developed!

Panel 1:

Hey, Peli? Are you home?

Tepi? Is that you? *OH JEEZ!* Visitors! My place is a total mess!

Kids, this is my friend *Pelinobius muticus*, the king baboon spider!

Oh gosh! Hi, I guess!

I was just about to tell them that tarantula venom isn't particularly dangerous to humans!

Panel 4:

Oh yeah! Why would we want to bite you in the first place? It is true that our bites can be kind of painful, but that's because our fangs are bigger.

Panel 5:

Old-world tarantulas are sometimes called aggressive, but a better term would be "defensive"! They will generally bite humans only when they feel threatened. Tarantulas usually prefer running away rather than trying to fight something much bigger than themselves!

Indian Ornamental Tarantula
Poecilotheria regalis
7–10 cm (2.76–3.94 in)

But when running isn't enough, new-world tarantulas have a special defense mechanism! Their abdomen is covered in a layer of special hairs that they may brush off at a predator when threatened.

Costa Rican Tiger Rump
Davus fasciatus

These hairs, called urticating hairs, can lodge themselves in the skin or eyes of an attacker, causing extreme irritation and pain. Their effectiveness varies depending on the species of tarantula.

Hey! Watch it, pal!

The Chilean rose tarantula, *Grammostola rosea*, has hairs that are only mildly irritating to humans.

Whereas the Brazilian whiteknee tarantula, *Acanthoscurria geniculata*, has hairs that can be extremely painful.

Antilles Pinktoe Tarantula
Caribena versicolor

Tarantulas may also use these hairs to mark territory. Some, like the tree-dwelling *Caribena* species, weave urticating hairs into their egg sacs to protect them against predators!

So spiders that are big and hairy are called tarantulas?

Tarantula originally referred to a specific wolf spider, *Lycosa tarantula*, named after the italian town of Taranto. It gradually became a term for any large spider!

Today it specifically means a spider who is a member of the family Theraphosidae. There are about a thousand species of tarantulas, and they're popular with people who like to keep spiders as pets!

There are a few reasons tarantulas make better pets than smaller spiders! They're much more shy and docile, and since their venom is so mild, accidental bites are less of a problem. They're mygalomorphs, as well, which means they live a lot longer!

Mexican Redknee Tarantula
Brachypelma hamorii

Speaking of big spiders, have you met *Theraphosa blondi* yet?

Ohhh, can we, Mom? I've only gotten to see them in books! *PLEASE PLEASE PLEASE?*

Hmmm, we can try! It is sort of on the way back...

Thanks, Peli! Sorry to chat and run, but there's still more to learn!

Have fun!

That water looks pretty nasty... Is electricity the only thing keeping us up?

The wind can be helpful too! Weather phenomena like a storm or a jet stream can take ballooning spiders huge distances as well!

Jet streams are giant, fast-moving air currents that are forming and dissipating at all times in our atmosphere. The biggest jet streams typically form at the borders of large masses of air when the two masses are drastically different temperatures, and ballooning spiders can get caught in them to travel massive distances!

SUBTROPICAL JET STREAM

POLAR JET STREAM

Looks like we'll be reaching South America soon. Let's aim for Peru!

Awww, I thought we were going to Brazil to see the Amazon rain forest!

The Amazon is here too! The great thing about Peru is there are a wide variety of climates spread across it. Monsoon seasons, cold and warm deserts, tropical and subtropical rain forests, and cool oceanic climates can all be found here, leading to a lot of biodiversity within a small area!

Roly Poly Orb-Weaver
Xylethrus scrupeus
Females 7.7–9.6 mm (0.30–0.37 in)
Males 4.5–4.8 mm (0.17–0.31 in)
This orb-weaver rolls itself up
into a tiny ball when threatened!

Two-Tailed Bark Spider
Neotama mexicana
Females 6.5–11.8 mm (0.25–0.46 in)
Males 6.1–8.2 mm (0.24–0.32 in)
The two "tails" on spiders
in the family Hersiliidae are
actually elongated spinnerets!

Brazilian Wandering Spider
Phoneutria nigriventer
Females 17–48 mm (0.66–1.88 in)
Males 18.5–31 mm (0.72–1.22 in)
This spider's venom is extremely
dangerous to humans, so give
them a wide berth!

**Thorned Heart
Orb-Weaver**
Micrathena clypeata
Females 8.6–10.3 mm (0.33–0.4 in)
Males 3.7–4.2 mm (0.14–0.16 in)
This thin heart-shaped spider is also
surrounded by lots of spikes, like a little
eight-legged metaphor for love.

111

Goliath birdeaters are big, but they aren't really harmful to humans! Their venom has been compared to a wasp sting, which would hurt, but in reality, humans are more dangerous to them!

In the last 50 years, over 20% of the Amazon has been deforested, mostly to make room for cattle for the beef and leather industries.

It continues to be clear-cut and burned at an accelerating rate, making up 14% of the annual deforestation across the globe.

Deforestation, pollution, and rising temperatures on earth, sometimes called global warming or climate change, are all leading to the destruction of spiders' natural habitats across the world.

GLOBAL WARMING

Greenhouse gases like CO_2 from coal or diesel, or methane from cow manure at industrial farms, are trapped in the atmosphere. Solar radiation that would normally bounce off the earth and leave our atmosphere is trapped by these gases and radiated back down, causing global temperatures to rise.

And massive changes for one animal means massive changes for all the animals around them. Every ecosystem on earth holds a delicate balance between every plant and animal that inhabits it!

Removing one species of spider can have a ripple effect that doesn't stop at the borders of that ecosystem! Animals that eat that spider suddenly have less food, and anything the spider eats will experience a huge population boom. Those changes then affect more plant or animal populations, and so on and so on.

Spiders collectively eat **880 MILLION TONS** of insects each year! That means they eat the weight of about 12,000 blue whales every single day!

KEEP 'EM COMIN'

And insects aren't just annoying! They can destroy crops, ruin gardens, damage homes, and more! Without spiders, humans would be overwhelmed by a never-ending swarm of bugs at all times!

Many of the insects that spiders eat are carriers of bacteria or disease as well, meaning that spiders actually help stop the spread of sickness!

Oooh, a buffet!

Mosquitoes can carry malaria, an infectious disease that can be fatal to humans.

Ticks can spread a serious infection called Lyme disease by biting.

And flies are capable of bringing a huge range of diseases to humans, like dysentery, cholera, and tuberculosis.

—GLOSSARY—

Abdomen
The abdomen, or opisthosoma, is the back segment of a spider's body, which contains its heart, silk glands, and important parts of its digestive system.

Aggregate
The sticky glue that holds prey captive when they make contact with an orb web.

Amino acids
Organic compounds that combine to form proteins and are often referred to as building blocks of life in the natural world.

Antivenom
May also be called antivenin or venom antiserum. A medication made to neutralize toxins in the bloodstream.

Arachnid
A classification of joint-legged invertebrate animals known as arthropods that includes spiders, ticks, mites, and scorpions.

Arachnologist
A person who studies arachnids.

Arachnophile
A person who loves spiders and/or other arachnids.

Araneomorph
A suborder of spider that is usually smaller in size and has chelicerae that move in a side-to-side pinching motion. Sometimes called Labidognatha.

Arthropod
An invertebrate animal from the phylum Euarthropoda, which includes all insects, arachnids, and crustaceans.

Biodiversity

A term referring to the wide variety of life-forms on earth, or sometimes just the species within a specific ecosystem or area.

Calamistrum

A row of special bristles on the legs of cribellate spiders used to comb bands of fuzzy silk out of the silk-spinning organ known as the cribellum.

Cephalothorax

The front segment of a spider's body, which contains its eyes and mouth opening. Sometimes called a prosoma.

Chelicerae

The front pair of appendages on a spider's body, which contain the fangs and often venom glands.

Cribellum

A plate covered in tiny holes that extrude many thin strands of silk, which are combed out by the specialized leg bristles known as calamistrum. Cribellate spiders are any spider that has a cribellum.

Exoskeleton

An external skeleton that protects the body of an animal, as opposed to an endoskeleton, like that of a human, which resides inside the body.

Gland

An organ inside an animal that synthesizes chemicals or substances for use inside the body or to be secreted outside the body.

Hemolymph

Invertebrates have hemolymph instead of blood. Blood (which is found in vertebrates) gets its red color from the interaction between iron and oxygen inside of the hemoglobin in red blood cells. But hemolymph is light blue because it contains hemocyanin, which contains copper instead of iron.

Hydrogel

A gel made up of polymers that are usually suspended in water. They are highly absorbent and have been used to create things like contact lenses and wound dressings.

Invertebrate
　　An animal without a backbone or
　　any kind of spinal column.

Larva
　　The first stage of life (after hatching) for an insect
　　before going through its metamorphosis to become
　　an adult.

Mesothelae
　　The closest living relatives of the first spiders on earth belong to
　　this dwindling suborder.

Mygalomorph
　　A suborder of spider that is usually larger in size and has chelicerae that
　　move in an up-and-down motion. Sometimes called Orthognatha.

Myrmecophily
　　A term for any species of organism, including plants and fungi, that
　　interact positively with ants or ant colonies.

Pedipalp
　　The second pair of appendages on a spider, on either side of the
　　chelicerae, which resemble shortened legs. Males have bulbs on the
　　end of their pedipalps, which is an easy way to visually differentiate
　　males and females.

Pheromones
　　Chemicals produced by an animal that affect the behavior of other
　　members of the same species.

Phototaxis
　　Bodily movement by an organism in response to changes in light.

Pigment
　　A material that reflects light at a specific wavelength, giving it color.
　　Melanin is an amino acid that is the pigment responsible for most skin
　　and hair coloration in humans.

Protein
　　A complex molecule made up of amino acids, one of the main
　　components of all organic tissue.

Seta
> A stiff, hairlike bristle usually found on invertebrates. Setae is the plural form.

Spinneret
> The organ on a spider and some insect larvae that produces silk.

Stabilimentum
> A wide silk structure built on some orb webs that may reflect UV light and provides camouflage for a spider.

Tapetum
> A reflective surface in the eye that helps increase available light and improves one's ability to see in dark conditions.

Toxin
> A poisonous, usually unstable substance produced by a living organism or a living cell.

Trichobothria
> Elongated setae found on arachnids and insects that can detect vibrations and electrical charges in the air.

Venom
> A poisonous substance secreted by animals and typically injected into prey or aggressors by biting or stinging.